Penguin Specials fill a gap. Written by some of today's most exciting and insightful writers, they are short enough to be read in a single sitting – when you're stuck on a train; in your lunch hour; between dinner and bedtime. Specials can provide a thought-provoking opinion, a primer to bring you up to date, or a striking piece of fiction. They are concise, original and affordable.

To browse digital and print Penguin Specials titles, please refer to **www.penguin.com.au/penguinspecials**

ALSO BY MARK O'NEILL

Tzu Chi: Serving with Compassion

*Frederick: The Life of My Missionary
Grandfather in Manchuria*

The Chinese Labour Corps:

The Forgotten Chinese Labourers of the First World War

MARK O'NEILL

PENGUIN BOOKS

Published by the Penguin Group
Penguin Group (Australia)
707 Collins Street, Melbourne, Victoria 3008, Australia
(a division of Penguin Australia Pty Ltd)
Penguin Group (USA) Inc.
375 Hudson Street, New York, New York 10014, USA
Penguin Group (Canada)
90 Eglinton Avenue East, Suite 700, Toronto, Canada ON M4P 2Y3
(a division of Penguin Canada Books Inc.)
Penguin Books Ltd
80 Strand, London WC2R 0RL, England
Penguin Ireland
25 St Stephen's Green, Dublin 2, Ireland
(a division of Penguin Books Ltd)
Penguin Books India Pvt Ltd
11 Community Centre, Panchsheel Park, New Delhi – 110 017, India
Penguin Group (NZ)
67 Apollo Drive, Rosedale, North Shore 0632, New Zealand
(a division of Penguin New Zealand Pty Ltd)
Penguin Books (South Africa) (Pty) Ltd
Rosebank Office Park, Block D, 181 Jan Smuts Avenue, Parktown North,
Johannesburg 2196, South Africa
Penguin (Beijing) Ltd
7F, Tower B, Jiaming Center, 27 East Third Ring Road North, Chaoyang
District, Beijing 100020, China

Penguin Books Ltd, Registered Offices: 80 Strand, London, WC2R 0RL,
England

First published by Penguin Group (Australia) in association with Penguin
(Beijing) Ltd, 2014

penguin.com.cn

ISBN: 9780143800316

CONTENTS

Preface

'The war in Europe is a matter that does not concern us, the Chinese people. We Chinese came to Europe as neutrals, to make a paltry living . . . a virtuous ruler's name will be remembered for 10000 generations, so why not halt your troops and select an auspicious location to build a palace of peace?'

These words written by a Chinese labourer named Yuan Chun are taken from the moving letter he sent to Kaiser Wilhelm II of Germany in an appeal to bring the bloody conflict of World War One to an end.

Yuan was one of some 135000 Chinese men who were sent to France and Belgium between 1916 and 1922 to help the Allied war effort. They loaded cargoes, dug trenches, filled sandbags, repaired tanks and artillery; they laid railway lines, repaired roads, built ports and aerodromes; they removed animal carcasses and ammunition from the battlefield, collected the bodies of the dead and built the graves to bury them.

The Chinese formed the largest contingent of foreign workers employed by the Allies during the war, outnumbering the Indians, black South Africans, Egyptians and West Indians, and constituting the first large-scale migration of Chinese to Europe. The 94 400 men who worked for the British Army joined the Chinese Labour Corps (CLC), the name most commonly used to describe these labourers. The remaining 40 000 worked for France – in its army and in its farms, mines and factories. Of this number, around 10 000 were 'lent' to help the American Expeditionary Forces. At war's end, the 3 000 workers who stayed behind founded the Chinese community in France.

The Chinese labourers' remarkable story is little known in Europe or China. History books describe the military campaigns involving tens of thousands of men that took place during World War One across Europe and the Middle East. They delve into the politics of the combatant countries, detail the horrific cost in human lives – more people died during the four-year conflict than in any previous war in history – and remark on the inability of national leaders to end the slaughter, 'lions led by donkeys' being a popular phrase used to describe the British infantry and the generals who commanded them. On China's role in World War One, however, the history books remain silent.

For almost a century the story of the Chinese labourers has remained a hidden page of the Great War, at most a mere footnote. The countries that recruited and transported the Chinese workers – Britain, France and Canada – went to great lengths to keep the operation secret. The men themselves left few records, but their story is as dramatic and extraordinary as the war's other participants.

The men were thousands of kilometres from home and had no connection to the conflict. For most of them, it was their first time outside China. The majority were illiterate and could not read Chinese, let alone French or English. They found themselves in a strange country, a short distance from a terrible war, living and working under dangerous conditions that were completely outside their previous experience. Each of them was there not to fight for their country but to earn a modest wage.

Around 3000 of the workers died from injuries sustained during bombing and shelling, from accidents caused by the unexploded ammunition they were clearing, and from diseases such as tuberculosis and Spanish influenza. At least 700 men died in German submarine attacks before they had even set foot in Europe.

The bodies of the Chinese men are buried in the two cemeteries that were set aside for them, and in military cemeteries in France and Belgium. The gravestones of some are broken and their names have been lost; few come to mourn them so far from home. Like all who took part in the terrible conflict, those who survived were scarred, physically and emotionally.

This book tells the story of these Chinese workers, their experiences in World War One and their contribution to the Allied war effort.

Raising the Corps

When World War One began on 28 July 1914, China's young republic was not yet three years old. For its leaders, the main priority was preventing the contagion of war from spreading to their own country, a real possibility since the combatants – Britain, France, Germany, Austro-Hungary and Russia – had concessions and economic interests in China. It was nominally an independent sovereign state, but in reality China was weak and dependent on other countries; it had twenty-seven foreign concessions, which would not allow customs tariffs to be raised above 5 per cent, and was still paying the crippling Boxer Indemnity of 450 million taels of silver to eight countries, a fee equivalent to more than US$6.5 billion today. By the time the indemnity was finally amortised, at the end of 1940, the fee would equal almost 1 billion taels of silver, including interest.

Eager to avoid exacerbating its position, on 6 August 1914 the Chinese government proclaimed its 'absolute neutrality during the European war' and forbade the foreign powers from engaging in hostilities on Chinese land or in its territorial waters. But where some saw danger, others saw opportunity. Would the war weaken the imperial powers and give China a chance to play a greater role in world affairs? If China joined the winning side, could it recover the concessions given to the Western powers, in particular those occupied by Germany in the eastern province of Shandong? And could China's involvement result in a reduction of the huge Boxer Indemnity?

Such thoughts were playing in the fertile brain of one Liang Shiyi, a senior adviser to President Yuan Shikai. In 1904 and 1905, Liang had helped to negotiate the treaty under which Britain recognised Chinese sovereignty over Tibet. He had also been Minister of Railways under the Qing government. These experiences gave Liang an understanding of foreign diplomacy that was rare among the leaders of the new republic. He was convinced that the British, French and Russian alliance would win the war, and did his utmost to persuade China's leaders to join the Allies in order to benefit from this potential victory.

Within weeks of the outbreak of war, Liang proposed to John Jordan, British Minister to China, that the two sides use 50000 Chinese troops to jointly attack an area known as the Jiaozhou Bay concession in Shandong, which Germany had occupied since 1898. In this way, China would both join the Allied side and reclaim part of its lost territories. Without consulting his French and Russian counterparts, Jordan rejected the idea outright. Britain believed the conflict would be short and that it did not need the support of China and its weak military. More importantly, perhaps, Britain was the world's largest imperial power and did not want to disturb the colonial order by forming an alliance with a semi-colonised country.

Britain's principal ally in East Asia was Japan, with whom it had signed a treaty in 1902. Japan was the only colonial power in China not directly involved in the conflict, and its leaders moved quickly to exploit the power vacuum caused by the Europeans' absence. In the first week of the war, Japan proposed to Britain that it would offer military assistance if it could take over German territories in the Pacific. In November 1914, in a swift and decisive operation, it attacked and captured the German-held city of Qingdao (Tsingtao), the most important city in Shandong. The manoeuvre enabled Japan to secure a firmer foothold in China and raised its standing in the eyes of the European powers.

In early 1915 Liang made a second proposal to the British, offering to send both workers and soldiers to fight on the Allies' side. The model he proposed was that of the 'Ever Victorious Army' of Chinese soldiers led by General Charles George Gordon and other British officers in the 1860s, which defeated the Taiping rebels. Once again, Liang's offer was rejected, due to strong opposition from Japan and from the British trade unions, which opposed the importation of Chinese labour.

His gambits rebuffed, Liang compromised by suggesting the idea of sending workers to Europe instead of soldiers. China's army and navy were insignificant compared to the giant armies fighting in France and on the Eastern Front, but manpower was something China had in abundance. The Allies were suffering heavy losses on the battlefield and their need for additional men was acute, if not on the front-line then working in arms factories, building roads, railways and bridges, and carrying out support work for the troops.

A major factor in the mind of Liang and his colleagues was the Twenty-One Demands presented by Japan to the Chinese government on 18 January 1915, insisting on wide-ranging rights and privileges for itself in China. After the government's initial rejection, Japan presented a slimmed-down Thirteen Demands, which Yuan's government accepted, and the two sides signed an agreement on 25 May 1915. Clearly, China needed the help of the Western powers to deal with Japan and regain the former German concessions in Shandong that Japan had taken over. It was also hoped that the Chinese workers would learn skills useful for their country's modernisation during their time abroad, and that their assistance would give China a place at the negotiating table at the end of the war.

So it was that in the early summer of 1915, the Chinese government offered to send a total of 300 000 workers to Britain and France to perform non-combatant duties.

Liang's persistence paid off, and in June France decided to accept the offer.

Poster for a film report on the Chinese Labour Corps

Recruitment by the French

The French Ministry of War had considered importing Chinese workers to assist France in its war effort as early as March 1915, but the idea was dropped. As the war intensified, however, and France was drawing more than 180 000 workers from its colonies, including Algeria, Morocco, Tunisia, Vietnam and Madagascar, it became clear that the country's growing need for manpower could not be satisfied.

Responding to China's offer of manpower, France sent a recruitment delegation headed by Georges Truptil, a retired lieutenant-colonel. China was still a neutral party at this stage, and in order to prevent German accusations that the country was breaching its neutrality, it was proposed that the Chinese labourers be recruited by 'private companies', and that Truptil should hide his identity by posing as a specialist in agricultural development.

To facilitate the recruitment drive, Liang Shiyi and the director of the Chinese Industrial Bank set up a private firm called the Huimin Company, to manage the hiring and maintain the pretence that this was a private operation. With its headquarters in Beijing, the company set up branches in Tianjin, Qingdao, Hong Kong and Pukou in Jiangsu province. A number of other private companies were also involved in the profitable business of recruiting, with men being hired in Guangxi, Yunnan, Sichuan and Shanghai, but the Huimin Company would remain the main recruiter. Over the next few years, the company hired a total of nearly 32 000 men, receiving a payment from the French of 100 francs per worker, with 50 francs being sent to each man's family.

In offering its manpower, the Chinese government laid down three conditions: the men would not take part in combat duties, they would receive the same rights and freedoms as French workers, and China reserved the right to send diplomats to ensure that the men's rights and freedoms were being respected. The memory was still fresh from the last fifty years of Qing-dynasty rule, when Chinese men had been sent to Cuba, Peru, the United States and South Africa as indentured labourers, and had encountered working conditions not far removed from slavery. The popular name for the workers was *maizhuzai*, meaning pigs that are sold, a term that aptly described their place in the social order. When the families of these men bid them farewell at the pier, they did not know if they would see their loved ones again.

The government did not want to see history repeat itself.

Truptil's arrival in Beijing on 17 January 1916 was followed by several months of negotiations to reach an agreement with the Huimin Company. On the French side, Truptil had to obtain a consensus from different branches of his government, notably the Ministry of War and the Ministry of Foreign Affairs, as well as from La Confédération Générale du Travail (CGT), the country's biggest trade union. The CGT was fearful that the Chinese would threaten the jobs of its members, if not during the war, then afterwards. As a result, it demanded a limit to their number and a fixed-term contract.

The resulting five-year contract was more favourable than that later offered by the British. Article One of the contract stated that, in order to preserve China's neutrality, the men must act as volunteers and civilians, working in factories or farms and not taking part in any work connected to the war. Although the contract stipulated that the Chinese workers would not be employed in military operations, it did not specify that they would be kept away from battle zones. The men were promised Sundays off and other rights enjoyed by French workers, and they received the same pay as their French colleagues. Importantly, the men were given the choice of remaining in France at the end of their service.

The contract included the promise of a daily minimum of 100 grams of rice, with the substitution of

European food if the workers agreed. On leaving China, they would receive two blue cotton shirts, two pairs of blue cotton trousers and one pair of padded trousers, as well as one straw mat and cooking utensils. If they were injured at work, the employer must pay for their treatment and compensate them. Article 15 stipulated that the employer must also protect the labourers from any maltreatment by workers of other nationalities.

On 14 May 1916, Truptil signed a contract to hire 50 000 workers, mainly sourced from the northern provinces; the men would be under the control of the *troupes coloniales*, part of the French War Ministry. In a report dated 16 April, the French military attaché in Beijing had written to his minister in Paris, saying that 'the Chinese workers, especially those from the north, must be satisfactory for us. They are sober, strong, hard-working and docile. They will adapt to our climate and the work, however tough, as long as it only requires physical labour.'

The first group of workers hired by France set sail from Tianjin in July 1916, accompanied by foreign missionaries and officers who spoke Chinese. Their route took them across the Indian Ocean, along the Suez Canal and through the Mediterranean, before arriving in Marseilles on 24 August.

The workers' long journey was the result of a simple economic decision: the wages on offer, for them and their families, were better than anything they could earn at home. But while the men had signed of their own free will, and not under the orders of their government, they had little or no knowledge of the war and its causes, or of the terrible slaughter of human life taking place on the battlefields of Europe. Most of the men were illiterate farmers or low-paid city workers; there was no radio or television to inform them of the horrors of the air raids and bombardments that many of them would soon be encountering. Nor was it in the interests of their recruiters to warn them of what lay ahead. With the death toll rising each week, the French were desperate for manpower.

The sinking of the Athos

The diplomats of Germany and the Austro-Hungarian Empire noted the number of workers visiting the French consulate to sign contracts, and were alarmed. From May 1916 the German Embassy in Beijing repeatedly protested to China's government, arguing that it was the same as sending soldiers to fight on the French side. The government responded by saying that the men were being employed by private contractors and that this did not mean a violation of China's neutrality: it was the right of their citizens to seek work abroad if they wished.

The Germans began distributing leaflets at the recruiting stations and publishing statements in their

Chinese-language publications, warning the applicants that promises of avoiding war zones were a deception and that their lives would be at risk due to air raids and bombardments. 'You will suffer the worst atrocities in the world and become the spirits wandering on the field of battle. You will never find your way home and can never be buried in your native land.' The leaflets reported that wages would be poor, and paid in a paper currency that was depreciating; for this, they would work long and exhausting hours and would live within range of the powerful German artillery.

The leaflets were also placed on board the ships transporting the workers to Europe, threatening that German submarines patrolling the Atlantic and Mediterranean would sink Allied ships, including unarmed vessels, without warning. The threat was realised on 17 February 1917, when the French steamship *Athos* was sunk by German submarines 200 nautical miles off the coast of Malta. The incident resulted in the loss of 754 lives, including 543 Chinese men who were destined to never set foot on European soil, and who would be the first Chinese casualties of the Great War. Among the dead was Robert Haden, a missionary of the American South Presbyterian Mission in Suzhou, who drowned while trying to save the life of a Chinese labourer.

Following this tragedy, the ships no longer travelled to Europe via the Suez Canal and Mediterranean. Instead, the workers were taken over the Pacific to Canada, across the country by train and then transported in ships across the Atlantic, accompanied by anti-submarine patrols. An alternative route travelled via Singapore, across the Indian Ocean, around the Cape of Good Hope, up the coast of West Africa, past Gibraltar to Marseilles. Both routes increased the trip from China by up to three months, making the already long journey far more unpleasant.

"ATHOS". – TORPILLÉ EN MM MÉDITERRANÉE LE 17 FÉVRIER 1917

The sinking of the Athos on 17 February 1917. More than 500 Chinese labourers drowned when the boat was torpedoed by a German submarine in the Mediterranean Sea

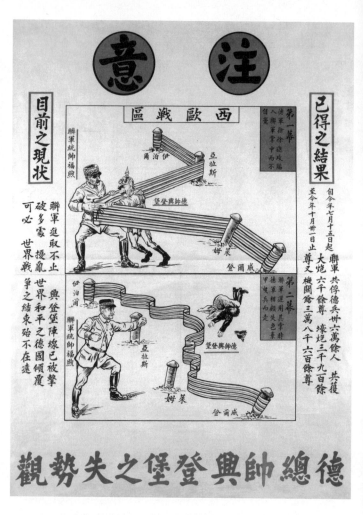

Chinese propaganda poster depicting the German emperor William II (*to the right*) and the French Field Marshall Ferdinand Foch (*left*)

The British Experience

Initially, the British declined the Chinese offer of manpower. The opposition of its trade unions was a key factor, as unemployment at home was high and the unions feared competition from China's cheap, efficient and non-unionised workers. A core principle of colonialism – the superiority of the coloniser over the colonised – was also at stake: if blacks and Asians were fit to fight and die for the Empire, why were they denied equal rights with white people at home? Furthermore, using Chinese workers would raise the status of China and risk giving it more rights as an Allied nation.

By the middle of 1916, however, these considerations had been swept aside by Britain's devastating losses on the battlefield, which put the very future of the country at risk. In the single month of July 1916, when the 141-day Battle of the Somme began, nearly 187000 British soldiers were killed, wounded or missing. The situation was dire, prompting David Lloyd George, Secretary of

State for War, to muse privately: 'We are going to lose this war.'

On 28 July, the British Army Council accepted the Chinese offer. With every able-bodied man needed on the battlefields, no white labour could be spared to do the work of supporting the army. Rejecting the long-established British colony of Hong Kong as a recruiting centre, the government selected Weihaiwei, on the eastern tip of Shandong, as the best choice. The diminutive Cantonese were considered unfit for the strenuous physical work required, and it was believed that the sturdy men of the north would be best able to adapt to the cold, wet climate and harsh winters of northern France and Belgium. Of the total of some 135 000 Chinese workers who came to Europe during World War One, 80 000 were from Shandong, where the vast majority of the male population were engaged in agriculture and accustomed to hard physical work.

For the British, the location seemed ideal. Britain had owned a lease on the port of Weihaiwei since 1 July 1898, and it was the summer station of the British Chinese Fleet. As the port was not considered Chinese territory, the recruitment of workers did not legally compromise China's neutrality in the war. In addition, Weihaiwei had served as a recruiting centre for the 'coolies' sent to the gold and diamond mines of South Africa in 1904, and the facilities built to support that operation were still in place.

To head the mission, the British appointed Thomas Bourne, a railway engineer with twenty-eight years of experience in China. Bourne arrived in Beijing on 28 October 1916, and three days later made the journey to Weihaiwei, where he set up office with six British staff, including a surgeon, twenty Chinese clerks and assistants, and twenty Chinese and Sikh guards.

Initially, the response to Britain's recruitment drive was slow, and by late November Bourne had recruited fewer than forty men. The Chinese were suspicious of being hired by the British Army, and of what awaited them on the other side of the world.

The paperwork the workers signed was simpler than the French contracts – one page, with English on one side and Chinese on the other. It stipulated that the men signed of their own volition, after the conditions had been made clear to them, and that the job would involve 'work on railways, roads, etc., and in factories, mines, dockyards, fields, forests etc. Not to be employed in military operations.' In return for the payment of just 1 franc a day, with their families at home receiving 10 Chinese silver dollars per month, they would work ten hours a day, seven days a week, with due consideration being given to Chinese festivals. A 'ganger', who was in charge of sixty men, would receive 1.5 francs a day and his family 15 dollars a month. Skilled workers earned more, with the highest wage of 5 francs a day going to interpreters and clerks who could speak English. In the case of death or total disability, the family would receive 150 Chinese silver dollars; for partial disability, the figure would be up to 75 Chinese silver dollars.

The contract was for three years, shorter than the French five-year term, and could be terminated at any time for misconduct or inefficiency on the part of the workers. Although the men were recruited as civilians, and would not wear military uniform, they were subject to military discipline and could be court-martialled, even executed.

The pay was low by British standards, but a guaranteed income for three years at this rate was considered a good wage for a Chinese labourer. Applicants were offered free food, clothing, medical care and accommodation, and passage home 'under all circumstances' at the end of their service. Unlike the French, the British stipulated that all Chinese workers had to be repatriated, largely because of pressure from Britain's strong trade union movement.

If the worker accepted these terms, he declared his name, age and home address. A clerk added these details to the paperwork, along with the seal of the British Emigration Bureau, and the worker then placed his inked thumb and fingerprint on the contract as signature.

Naked and disinfected

The Chinese government was closely involved in drawing up the contracts, but the recruitment drive continued to fail. In January 1917, the Chinese Foreign Ministry sent an offer of assistance to London. The three conditions outlined by the government revealed how closely China's offer of manpower through the CLC was linked to its diplomatic objectives: Britain would help China secure a seat at the postwar peace conference; it would allow a fifty-year delay in the payment of the Boxer Indemnity, with no increase in interest; and it would immediately allow China to raise taxes. Ultimately, Beijing's gift of manpower through the CLC would achieve none of these conditions.

In Britain, the existence of the CLC had been kept secret even from Parliament, known only to a small number of military and diplomatic officials. The first public announcement of its existence had occurred on 15 November 1916, when the official *London Gazette* reported that Lieutenant Colonel Bryan Fairfax of the Liverpool Regiment had been appointed its commander. Fairfax had served in China during the Boxer Rebellion, and also in South Africa. In July 1916 he had led his battalion in the Battle of the Somme, where he was gassed and invalided home. In 1917 he returned to France to set up the headquarters of the CLC.

Slowly, British recruitment gathered pace, largely

due to word of mouth and the extensive colonial network in place. Of the foreign powers in China, Britain had the largest footprint in terms of business, schools, mission stations and industry. The missionaries were the most effective recruiters, having the best access to potential applicants. Rare among foreigners, they lived among the ordinary Chinese, the farmers, carpenters, blacksmiths, stonemasons, brickmakers and bricklayers, and they spoke their language. Eventually, tens of thousands applied to join the CLC, persuaded by the combination of poverty, a surplus of labour and China's political instability.

On their first day as members of the CLC, applicants were told to remove their clothes and stand naked in line while a British soldier doused them with disinfectant. Medical officers then checked the men for twenty-one diseases, including bronchitis, malaria, tuberculosis, bad teeth, venereal diseases and trachoma, a contagious disease of the eyelids common in Shandong. Particular attention was paid to infectious diseases, because, if brought to France, their effect could be devastating. Between 30 per cent and 60 per cent of applicants were rejected on medical grounds, mainly due to trachoma. Most of those who were accepted were aged between twenty and forty.

After signing his employment contract with his fingerprint and thumbprint, the worker received an aluminium bracelet stamped with a five-digit serial number, which was sealed with metal rivets around his wrist. Along with the serial number was his name, in romanised letters and Chinese characters. Those who did not know their name or surname gave the village where they lived, their nickname, or the details of the person to whom they wished the Chinese portion of their pay to be sent. This became their 'name' for the next three years. The bracelet had to be worn at all times, and could only be removed after they returned to China. In combination, the bracelet, fingerprint and thumbprint worked as an administratively efficient means of identification, but it was considered insulting to many Chinese, who felt like criminals being registered on their way to prison.

Processing at Cangkou

In January 1917, the recruitment station at Weihaiwei was joined by another at Cangkou, on the Shandong railway. The centre was housed in a large abandoned silk factory that had been formerly used by the Germans and lay 15 kilometres north of the large port of Qingdao, where ocean liners could dock. Qingdao was under the control of Britain's ally, the Japanese, who with British help had seized it from the Germans in November 1914.

Cangkou soon became the more important recruitment centre, and for the next fourteen months the complex processed thousands of men. In his memoirs,

Sir Alwyne Ogden, a British diplomat who worked as an administrator for the CLC program, wrote: 'Coolies came from all over North China, and especially during Chinese New Year; they would come back from working in the fields of Manchuria for their annual holidays and very often when they saw our advertisements and heard of the prospects they would come in perhaps 100 miles or more to our recruitment office'. While most applicants came from Shandong and Hebei, others arrived from Liaoning, Jilin, Jiangsu, Hubei, Hunan, Anhui and Shanxi provinces.

'It was told tonight in the mess that the coolies do not know and do not question where they are going,' wrote Daryl Klein, a second lieutenant in the CLC, in January 1918. 'Having been assured that they are not going into action on the Western Front, they set out lightheartedly, as men on some fine adventure, not caring about their destination so long as they are fed and clothed.' Klein joined the CLC in late 1917, and was one of thirteen officers escorting a group of 4200 workers, along with five interpreters and one medical assistant, who left Qingdao in February 1918 to travel to France, via Canada. He published an account of his experiences in his book, *With the Chinks*.

Applicants were examined at Cangkou, and those selected were fed, clothed and equipped before being taken by train to Qingdao. The workers received several weeks' training in preparation for their long journey. Aided by Chinese guards, British NCOs drilled the men and emphasised the importance of personal cleanliness and tidiness. The men washed in large communal bathing stalls and their heads were shaved; pigtails, compulsory in the Qing dynasty, were cut off. The workers were issued with two sets of blue cotton suits for the summer and a set for winter, including woollen trousers, a cardigan, waistcoat, brown canvas raincoat and a felt hat with ear flaps and a copper badge stamped with the initials CLC.

Each group of fifteen men chose a leader, who was more literate and received a higher level of pay, and wore a chevron on his sleeve. The men received three meals a day, including rice, vegetables and fish, with meat served twice a week, along with plentiful supplies of tea. The free clothes and food, of better quality than they were accustomed to, made a good impression and increased the men's sense of wellbeing.

On 18 January 1917, three months after Britain's CLC recruitment drive had begun, the first contingent of 1088 workers was ready. After two weeks of drilling and preparation, the men were taken to the docks at Qingdao for their departure. There they saw things they had never seen in their life and could not have imagined – the huge vessels that would take them across the ocean.

Before departing, the men were sprayed once again with disinfectant, and their serial numbers and identity bracelets were checked a final time. As they boarded the ship, accompanied by six officer candidates, a doctor and a regular army captain, firecrackers were let off to lend a sense of celebration to their departure.

The wheelbarrows and push carts the men were allowed to take on board would prove useless in the mud and dust of Flanders and Picardy, but the musical instruments they were also permitted, such as drums, flutes and zithers, became their main source of relaxation on the long voyage and in the evenings in camp in France and Belgium.

No rest for the nervous

By late April 1917, the British had sent 35 000 labourers to work on the battlefields of Europe. When the last batch of nearly 2000 men left China in March 1918, the British had recruited 94 400 Chinese workers, a far larger number than those sent to work for the French, who would send around 40 000 men during the war. This figure was less than half the original target of 100 000 set by Paris, largely due to a lack of shipping, a problem that similarly prevented the British War Council from recruiting their targeted figure of 150 000 labourers.

Most of the men hired by the British sailed to Europe in the Canadian Pacific Line's *Empress of Russia* or

Empress of Asia. Following the sinking of the *Athos* in February 1917, the route took the men from China via the Japanese ports of Nagasaki, Yokohama or Moji, to take in supplies of coal, food and water, across the Pacific Ocean to Canada. The Chinese labourers were accommodated in cramped and poorly ventilated holds below deck, set apart from the ship's European passengers. Klein wrote: 'The coolies are not passengers capable of finding each his cabin; the coolies are so much cargo, livestock, which has to be packed away, so many head in a hold'.

Those who felt this discrimination most strongly were the translators, who could speak English and had mixed with the 'Big-Noses' in China or overseas. They were entitled to better accommodation and food than the workers but found the lowest-ranking British squaddie enjoyed more living space than they. When one ship reached Japan and docked for six days, the British went onshore for rest and recreation but the 2000 Chinese workers were ordered to remain on board, confined to a narrow space in stifling heat, with little air and poor hygiene. Klein also described how, during a voyage across the Pacific, a worker who stole a handful of peanuts during the night was court-martialled; he was handcuffed to a winch for six hours, with a notice explaining his crime, as a warning to others.

Few of the men had been to sea before, let alone

crossed an ocean, and many suffered from seasickness. Conditions didn't improve when they reached Vancouver after their three-week journey across the Pacific Ocean. Canada did not welcome Chinese workers and imposed a 'head tax' of C$500 on those who entered the country – equivalent to ten years' wages for an ordinary worker. To avoid paying the tax, the men were forced to wait on their crowded ships at William Head, outside Vancouver. It was an uncomfortable delay of several days, and in some cases several weeks, before they could be put into railway carriages for the journey across the country.

Vancouver had the largest Chinese community of any Canadian city, numbering 3559 in the census of 1911. After the outbreak of war, the Chinese community had showed their patriotism by buying C$100000 in war bonds, despite an unemployment rate of more than 50 per cent, and some Chinese served in the Canadian infantry that fought on the Allied side. Despite the efforts of the authorities to prevent any contact between the CLC workers and the resident Chinese, the locals spoke to the men while their boxcars were parked in Vancouver, and passed food to them. The men were not allowed to leave the trains' locked carriages, and were kept under armed guard. The windows were blackened, due to fear of opposition from Canadians who did not want Chinese crossing their country, and no bedding was provided.

Once under way, the train journey took eight days and nights to reach the port of Halifax in the eastern province of Newfoundland, 9000 kilometres away. The workers were not allowed to alight during stops, even for exercise, ensuring that they passed through Canada but did not 'enter' it, and so had no need to pay the head tax. The Canadian government went to great lengths to keep the operation secret, imposing a news blackout and ordering the railway workers not to speak of their cargo. When a group of people took photographs of dozens of workers being transferred from their boat into trains in Vancouver, the censor – a former journalist – ordered the police to seize the pictures. Despite their best efforts, the Canadian censors could not prevent American papers including *The Seattle Times* and *San Francisco Examiner* from publishing stories on the movement of the workers.

The government also intercepted communications from the Chinese consulate in Vancouver, along with any personal mail addressed to people in Canada with Chinese names. The fear was that Canada's Chinese citizens might try to persuade the men not to go to France and to remain in Canada. Letters to and from Chinese Canadians that were intercepted by the government showed that they knew what was going on. One, from Lee Kaun Sit of Vancouver, told his friend On Yick in Guangdong: 'The Allies are going all over China to encourage people to work for them. If they listen to them, they will endure all kinds of suffering. More than 10 000 Chinese work close to the battle front in Russia. The thousands of Chinese who arrive on the *Empress* boats in France will suffer the same fate.' Another wrote to his colleagues in Shanghai: 'Several thousand people from Shandong are arriving by steamer and will be sent to the front in France. They are certain to die.'

Between March 1917 and March 1918, a total of 84 000 Chinese workers crossed the length of Canada by train on their way to Europe. In Halifax, on the east coast, the men disembarked to enter a camp that was fenced in with barbed wire and guarded by armed soldiers. From there, they boarded troop ships and passenger vessels taken over by the government for the last and most dangerous leg of their long journey across the Atlantic Ocean, escorted by anti-submarine patrols. The workers had to wear lifejackets, and at night any form of light was banned, so as not to attract the submarines.

Klein wrote: 'Life was dreadfully restricted. The coolies had to wear the lifebelts at all times. All portholes were painted and then sealed up. The air in the holds became suffocating; when one man complained, a sergeant replied: "It is better that one man die than four thousand perish." Their convoy is protected only by a small gunboat. In the submarine zone, the coolest may be caught unawares,' Klein continued. 'It is a zone of perils and surprises, adventures and heroisms and eminently a zone of false alarms. There is no rest for the nervous. For the imaginative, it is a nightmare. For good and bad, it is upsetting.'

The two long ocean voyages and crowded, uncomfortable conditions were a great ordeal for the workers, especially when storms were encountered with waves several metres high. Klein described what he saw below deck during one voyage: 'I went down into one of the bunkholds amidships, where an odd 150 of my company are quartered. I could hear the groans before I got down to them. Like a house of mild torture. The majority had collapsed. A few, their strength suddenly gone, lay on the boarded floor, unable to climb into their bunks. It was a spectacle of weakness.'

Some of the men could not endure the seasickness and discomfort, and took their own lives by diving into the sea. There are no figures on the number of suicides in the official Chinese account. It is only stated that 700 died as a result of German submarine attacks, including those on the *Athos*.

Arriving in Britain, some ships docked at Liverpool or Plymouth, from where the workers were taken by train to Folkestone and then by ship to the headquarters of the CLC in Noyelles-sur-Mer, in Picardy, northern France. Other ships sailed directly to Boulogne, Le Havre and other French ports.

The loading of Chinese labourers at Weihaiwei in Shandong

No Horsemeat

Just before the first Chinese workers arrived in Marseilles in August 1916, *L'Excelsior* newspaper reported that the men, mostly from northern China, had been through a careful selection procedure. 'They will be able to endure our climate better than people from Annam [Vietnam]. Medical checks have shown that the vast majority are in excellent physical shape. Their arrival is good news for our continuing recruitment.'

Unlike the British, who used the Chinese exclusively to support their troops on the front-line in France and Belgium, the French put the labourers to work in the country's factories, both state-owned and private, as the terrible casualties on the front had led to serious shortages of labour in industry. The Chinese men joined the large-scale workforce of women and men from the French colonies who were sent off to help manufacture munitions, ships, aircraft, metal goods and petrochemicals. They also assisted in construction projects in cities across the country, from Dunkirk in the north to Brest in the northwest and Lyon, Saint-Étienne and Toulouse in the south. They helped unload cargo in ports and warehouses, worked in mines, and toiled in the fields and forests.

According to official Chinese reports, 23 166 labourers worked in areas away from the front-line. Making up 58 per cent of the 40 000 Chinese labourers who were transported to France, these men lived in camps or barracks, usually on the outskirts of cities, and were escorted to and from work by soldiers, as were the other foreign workers. These were the most fortunate of the labourers. Since they were far from the fighting, they were not exposed to German artillery or bombing. After they had finished work, they could go where they wished, free to visit the cafes, restaurants and brothels in the surrounding towns and cities.

Although the contracts the men had signed promised that their employer would treat them in the same way as their French employees, the living conditions and diet were poor. There was a severe shortage of interpreters, resulting in linguistic and cultural misunderstandings, and conflicts over work habits and customs. Most of their factory colleagues and townspeople regarded them with curiosity and xenophobia; some shop owners refused to sell them cigarettes. The men were given inferior clothing and served a foreign diet that included horsemeat. In October 1917, a man called Li Jun spoke on behalf of the workers when he complained that Chinese did not eat horsemeat, and if they were forced to, they would make trouble. The meat was removed at once from the menu.

The men's contracts also stipulated that they would receive the same pay as their European colleagues, but this was not always the case. Salaries were established directly between employer and worker, varying from 1 to 5 francs a day. The men were farmers, used to a hard life and long hours working on the land, but they had no experience of working in a factory or as part of a large team, and had little understanding of the war.

Several Chinese workers died in the French factories, due to accidents, disputes and illnesses that were not properly treated. Between 1916 and 1918, the men were involved in twenty-five strikes or violent demonstrations. There were arguments among themselves, usually related to gambling, and clashes with other foreign workers. In January 1917, in a gunpowder factory in Bassens, a brawl with Arab workers left two Chinese dead. A few days later, at a gunpowder factory in Bergerac, 500 Chinese attacked 250 Algerians; one Chinese was killed and sixty people were injured.

The protests were a result of poor working conditions, non-payment of wages, being assigned work that was not in their contracts and maltreatment, physical or verbal, by their overseers. Misunderstandings between the men and their overseers and other foreign workers were commonplace due to linguistic and cultural barriers and the lack of interpreters; a small incident could explode into violence involving dozens of people. In February 1917, 100 Chinese labourers on the Paris–Orleans railway line at Perigueux went on strike to protest over pay. Five months later, two labourers working on the railway at Saint-Barthélemy-le-Plain, in the central southern region of the country, attempted to derail a train.

Another grievance that led to violent protest was the men's anger at having to work near the front-line, within range of German artillery and bombers. Their contract specified that they would not be employed in military operations, and they therefore did not expect to be placed at risk of enemy attack. The most dramatic example came in 1917, when 500 Chinese labourers at a steel plant near Dunkirk refused to work because of the constant danger of German air raids. When the police arrived to restore order, they were met with a hail of bricks and they began firing their pistols in the air. According to the official report of the incident, the workers were not in the least intimidated. For them, armed French policemen were a less frightening prospect than German bombers. However, the situation changed to tragedy when the police began shooting at the Chinese workers, killing one and injuring six.

The French and other foreign workers regarded the labourers with fear and animosity, while the Chinese workers complained of the violence used against them by their employers and agents of the state. On 1 March 1918, Prime Minister Georges Clemenceau was forced to issue the following warning to regional and local commanders of the workers: 'It has come to my attention that the Chinese workers have been victim of brutality on the part of those who guard them. It should not be necessary to bring your attention to the unacceptable character of this, the seriousness and the consequences which it could have.' He repeated the warning that those who used the crop or baton against the workers would be punished.

While some labourers were treated with suspicion, others were able to mix with the local population. They worked in factories alongside the French women who had been mobilised in large numbers to replace the men sent to the front. There was a severe shortage of fit French men, and the Chinese were young and healthy. In some cases, romances developed.

This outcome had been predicted by the Minister of Justice, who sent a confidential letter to the Mayor of Saint-Fons on 26 July 1916, before the first ship had reached France, warning against marriages between French women and men from China or from the African colonies. 'If they have children, this will bring grave consequences both for the children and for the mothers. First, the children would lose the identity of a French person and, by their strange name, if they remain in France, would keep for the mother for ever the memory of a passing liaison with a native. We cannot legally oppose such unions.' Motivated by both a sense of racial purity and the problem of nationality of children born out of mixed unions, he advised the mayors to 'bring discreetly to the attention of the mothers of these half-breed children his concerns and make them realize the unfortunate consequences of these liaisons'.

China declares war

On 14 March 1917, China broke diplomatic relations with Germany. In exchange, the Allies agreed that it would suspend payment of indemnities until the end of hostilities. China declared war on Germany and Austro-Hungary on 14 August 1917, four months after the United States joined the conflict. As with its offer of manpower to the Allies two years earlier, China's main objective was to earn a seat at the bargaining table after the war and win back the German areas in Shandong, now occupied by Japan.

The declaration of war was not an easy decision for China, and opinion among the leadership and general public was divided. Those in favour argued that this was the moment to regain the territory that had been lost over many decades, as the United States was admired as the most generous of the big powers towards China. The arguments for those supporting neutrality were equally strong. In the spring and summer of 1917, it was not clear which side was going to win the war. If Germany won, what revenge would it exact against China? And if the Allies won, would they favour Chinese demands over those of Japan? International diplomacy was a matter of national interests and benefits, not justice and fairness.

The case for neutrality was well summarised by Kang You-wei, one of the leading reformers of the late Qing dynasty:

'The breach between the US and Germany is no concern of ours. If we analyse the public opinion of the country, we find that all people – high and low, well-informed and ignorant – betray great alarm when informed of the proposal to declare war on Germany, fearing that such a development may cause grave peril to the country.

'Which side will win the war? I shall not attempt to predict here. But it is undoubted that all the arms of Europe, and the industrial and financial strength of the US and Japan, have proved unavailing against Germany. On the other hand, France has lost her northern provinces; and Belgium, Serbia and Romania are blotted off the map. Should Germany

be victorious, the whole of Europe – not to speak of a weak country like China – would be in great peril of extinction. Should she be defeated, Germany still can – after the conclusion of peace – send a fleet to war against us. And, as the Powers will be afraid of a second world war, who will come to our aid? Have we not seen the example of Korea? There is no such thing as an army of righteousness which will come to the assistance of weak nations.'

After China's declaration of war against Germany, the French felt comfortable in moving more of the Chinese labourers closer to the front, in order to perform war-related duties similar to those carried out by Britain's CLC taskforce.

Many of the Chinese men working near the front were traumatised by the war – the incessant bombardments, the airplanes flying overhead, the endless noise of trucks and trains. They were men used to the rough and tiring working conditions of life in the countryside of Shandong and Hebei, but nothing had prepared them for living close to the front. On 23 May 1918, near Britain's CLC headquarters at Noyelles-sur-Mer in Picardy, a number of Chinese workers fled during a bombardment, climbing over a barbed-wire fence. They were found several days later, hungry, haggard and half-mad, wandering lost in the countryside.

In early 1918, discussions between France and China began on the establishment of a Chinese Expeditionary Force of 40 000 men to work as sappers at the front. Made up of volunteers from the regular army and labourers from the north of China, they would be under Chinese command, with a French officer working with each battalion. Both countries were keen on the project, which was supported by other members of the Allied coalition.

The first contingent of 10 000 was supposed to leave China at the end of February 1918, but the force never set out. The Allies could not provide the ships needed to transport the men, and the Americans did not provide the loans needed to equip them.

Working for the Russians and Americans

Between the end of 1915 and 1922, around 200 000 Chinese labourers also went to work in Russia, which had suffered enormous losses in the fighting as an ally of Britain and France. Chinese workers had previously been concentrated in the Far East region, but during the war they spread all over the country, including the Murmansk railway in the far northwest, the Baku oil-fields in the Black Sea and the steelworks and coalmines of the Donets basin in southeast Ukraine. Like the workers for France, they were recruited by private companies in order to maintain the appearance of China's neutrality.

Many of these workers would have a bitter experience in Russia. Their Russian employers and the Chinese middlemen did not honour their contracts and left them inadequately paid, clothed and fed, and without the money promised to them to return home. Many froze to death during the construction of the Murmansk railway during the bitter winter, when temperatures fell to minus 20 degrees Celsius. Their difficulties were compounded by the Russian Revolution of 1917 and the civil war that followed. Their poor living and working conditions pushed many Chinese to join the Bolshevik Red Army. Many of those who left China for Russia never returned.

The United States also needed thousands of workers to assist its army. In addition to workers from Europe, Indo-China and North Africa, the US requested 50000 labourers from the French, who provided 10000 Chinese. By August 1918, this number had increased to nearly 12000. The men's main task was to move munitions and dig trenches, and they continued to work for the Americans until May 1919, when they returned to French control.

The Chinese labourers working for the French were generally more fortunate than those employed by the British and Americans. Jiang Ting-fu, who worked with the Chinese labourers during the war and later became a well-known educator, commented: 'The Chinese labourers with the French were more contented than those with the British. Besides discipline, the difference in the attitude of the officers toward the labourers was also an important factor. Being much less race conscious, they were more democratic in their manner and took a more paternalistic interest in their labourers . . . the British officers stood on their dignity as officers, and perhaps as white men, most of the time.'

'Of the three armed forces [British, French and American], the Chinese seemed least willing to work for the latter,' wrote Xu Guoqi in his excellent book *Strangers on the Western Front*. 'They considered them stingy compared with the French and believed that the Americans made them work longer hours.'

Even less than the French and British, the Americans had made no preparations to manage this army of foreigners. There were disputes between the Americans and the French over the terms of contracts. The American officers treated the Chinese poorly and were unpopular. In one typical case of misunderstanding, the Chinese workers downed tools when an American officer said to a group of men, 'Let's go' – in Chinese, the word *'gou'* means 'dog'.

Chinese labourer Song Xiufeng poses with local boy Maurice Matton in Proven, Belgium

Chinese labourers at work in the Tank Corps' Central Workshops in Erin, France

Working for the British

When Britain's first contingent of Chinese labourers arrived in early April 1917, the army had a system in place to receive them. The British had selected Noyelles-sur-Mer, a commune in the Somme *department* of Picardy in northern France, to host the headquarters of the CLC. On the English Channel, it lay 100 kilometres from the site of the Battle of the Somme, the most devastating engagement of the war. Though somewhat isolated, the large camp established for the workers was not far from the front-line, with a railway line nearby.

The nearby port of Étaples became the principal depot and camp for the British Expeditionary Force, its largest in France, with 100 000 people and twenty hospitals spread over 12 square kilometres. Nineteen other camps were set up in the Pas-de-Calais region, the most important centre for the British Army during the war.

In addition to the camp at Noyelles-sur-Mer, the British also set up numerous temporary camps, closer to the locations where the men were put to work. Each camp housed up to 3000 workers, in barracks or tents. Four hospitals were established for the Chinese, the largest being at Noyelles-sur-Mer. With 1500 beds, the hospital was well equipped and staffed with Chinese-speaking doctors and Chinese dressers to nurse the sick. The workers received the same care and attention as the British soldiers, with facilities including x-ray machines and operating rooms, separate compounds for trachoma patients and those with other eye diseases and injuries, an isolation wing for those with infectious diseases and a large compound for the treatment of those who had lost their mind under the stress of war. It also had a detention centre. To give a flavour of home, each ward had a canary and a model pagoda several metres high stood near the main entrance, with a gong that struck the hours of the day. Though thousands of kilometres from the mother-land, it was the largest Chinese hospital in the world.

The commander of the CLC, Colonel Bryan Fairfax, lived and worked in the Château de Fransu in the town; another building served as a residence for the officers, while the non-commissioned officers (NCOs) used the Hôtel des Voyageurs. In contrast, the Chinese labourers lived and worked under military discipline, housed in camps surrounded by barbed wire and guarded by armed soldiers. As non-combatants, the Chinese men were not armed. They slept in barracks or large tents, with fifty beds to a room, and were not allowed to use the same toilets as the British soldiers, largely to prevent the spread of trachoma. The labourers worked ten hours a day, seven days a week, except for traditional Chinese holidays, and were organised into companies of 500 men. Of these, twenty-four were British officers and NCOs, led by a major or captain. The key members of the unit were the 'gangers', the Chinese overseeing the men under the command of a British officer. These men were critical to the efficient operation of their work unit, as the labourers worked best under the supervision of the ganger, with little interference from the Europeans. The interpreters also played a critical role in the management and operations of the CLC; they were the principal means of communication between the men and the gangers and the officers who commanded them.

The men provided manual labour and ran truck and motorcycle repair shops, smith and paint shops to serve the British military units on the front-line. They played an important role in maintaining tanks for the Battle of Cambrai, which lasted from 20 November to 7 December 1917. Digging trenches was another of their most important tasks. The British had a total of 9600 kilometres of trenches, and the Chinese could dig them faster than the Indian workers or British squaddies. They were not allowed on the front-line, however, where the trenches were dug by British soldiers.

The men ate two meals a day, before and after work, prepared by Chinese cooks from rice, meat or dried fish, vegetables, tea, nut oil, salt, flour and margarine. The gangers and interpreters, many of them students, received better food than the ordinary workers. Most workers were careful with their money and the British set up a savings bank for them; it remained open until August 1918, and collected more than 14 million francs.

Good workers – but no fraternising

The British Army actively worked to prevent any relations, civil or military, between the Chinese and Europeans. In *Notes on Chinese Labour*, published on 2 August 1918 by the CLC, the Controller of Labour stated that British officers should not become familiar with Chinese because it 'caused a loss of prestige and a much decreased efficiency . . . Undue familiarity between any white personnel and Chinese employee was to be deprecated as subversive of discipline.'

The labourers needed a pass to leave their barracks, and were not allowed to mix socially with anyone outside – be they Allied soldiers, other foreign workers or French people. Outside the camp, they had to wear their uniform and a cap, so they could be easily recognised. The men were subject to strict military discipline, including corporal punishment and prison in the case of strikes. If they were late or absent from work or insulted their superiors, they had to pay a fine.

To the British, these restrictions were necessary due to the military urgency of the situation and the need to use the men in the most productive way possible. As the world's biggest empire, Britain had experience of managing large numbers of people but never such an army of Chinese. The labourers posed different and more complex problems than the armies of people from the colonies, with whom the military was more familiar. From an administrative point of view, keeping the men in a closed camp was the most cost-efficient means of managing the workers.

It was recognised that the Chinese men were good workers. In November 1919, the Controller of Labour wrote a report to the Quartermaster General about the foreign workers used by the British Army during the war. He rated the Chinese highly, saying that the Indians did not well endure the cold winter of northern France and black South Africans could not be used in dangerous areas. 'Chinese labour, properly handled, was undoubtedly most efficient; the extensive systems of defence organised in the rear at the time of the enemy offensive in 1918 could not have been completed in the time were it not for the excellent work of the CLC.'

The Controller's *Notes on Chinese Labour* of August 1918, which was distributed to British officers, reported that the Chinese were very hardy men and, properly handled, were among the best labourers in the world. 'It is astonishing what the coolie is capable of . . . one party (of six men) excavated at the rate of 230 cubic feet of chalk and flint and about one foot of surface soil per man per eight hours.' The Controller certified 4725 Chinese as highly skilled in the manufacture of tanks, light railways and wagons, and doing other specialised jobs.

Praise also came from Marshal Ferdinand Foch, the French general who was commander-in-chief of Allied forces in 1917 and 1918. 'They were first-class workers who could be made into excellent soldiers, capable for exemplary bearing under modern artillery fire.' Manico Gull, the British commander of the second group of CLC workers, went so far as to say that 'their emigration from the shores of Shandong takes its place certainly as one of the most important aspects of the Great European War'. Gull's opinion was exaggerated perhaps, to meet the needs of wartime propaganda, but he expressed the view held by most commanders. An article published in *L'Information* newspaper in June 1918 commented: 'Of all the foreign workers employed in France, it is the yellow ones which have been the most satisfactory. All the reports of the employers agree on this point. The Chinese thrives in different weathers, he is patient and attentive; he works without stopping. Those from the North are very strong.'

Revolt and mutiny

The Chinese labourers working for the British faced the same obstacles as those working for the French. One difficulty was a chronic shortage of interpreters, with as few as five in a camp of 4200. A documentary broadcast by the state China Central Television in May 2009 reported that misunderstandings led to minor issues escalating out of proportion. 'In some cases, British guards opened fire, killing Chinese workers. They were subject to strict military discipline, with punishments including being tied up to trees. The British criticised the French for their gentler treatment of the workers, allowing them to mix with the local population. The British said that the French should treat them in the same way as they did.'

To address the issue, the British Army printed a phrasebook for staff manning the camps, which included such statements as 'I want eight men to go over there very quickly', 'Why do you not eat this food?', 'The inside of this tent is not very clean', 'You must have a bath tomorrow'.

The shortage of interpreters meant that when the workers had a complaint and their British officer or NCO could not understand them, the response could be punishment, with officers sometimes opening fire. This led to resentment, injury and even death. In one YMCA report, a lieutenant in charge of 1000 men was reported as hitting the workers on the face, kicking them and calling them names; in turn, they cursed him and finally a strike occurred. The guards opened fire and four workers were killed.

While their contract had promised that they would not be employed in military operations, many men found themselves at the same risk as soldiers. On 4 and 5 September 1917, fifteen Chinese men were killed and twenty-one wounded in the German bombing of Dunkirk and Boulogne. On the night of 18 May 1918, at least fifty men were killed in a German air raid. More died during the German bombing of their camps on 30 July that year; others who fled strongly resisted being taken back to the camp and were taken to another further away from the front. There were also stories of Chinese men killing German prisoners of war with grenades, in retaliation for the deaths of their comrades.

In July and September 1917, Chinese labourers working at a steel plant in Leffrinckoucke, close to the Belgian border, went on strike after bombings by German planes and fled into the countryside. One of the biggest revolts occurred in September 1917, following a mutiny by British soldiers in Étaples: 1000 squaddies broke out of their camp and marched through the neighbouring town of Le Touquet, which was out of bounds to them. The mutiny was put down by soldiers from an artillery company and the Machine Gun Corps.

When news of the mutiny reached Chinese and Egyptian labourers working at the port of Boulogne, they went on strike to protest their working conditions, poor food, bad treatment and the risk of German bombing. The men entered the city and attempted to loot a hotel and café, before being driven away. They then attacked a club used by army officers. Soldiers opened fire, killing and wounding a large number of men and arresting others.

The contrast with the punishments given to the British mutineers was sharp. Only one Briton was executed for attempted mutiny; three men received ten years' penal servitude, ten were sentenced to one year in prison with hard labour, and thirty-three received between seven and ninety days' field punishment.

According to Brian Fawcett in his excellent *Chinese Labour Corps in France 1917–1921*, there were several mutinies. On 10 October 1917, five men were killed and fourteen wounded after a dispute over discipline. On 16 December 1917, there was a mutiny at Les Fontinettes because of bullying by British NCOs. An armed guard killed four Chinese and wounded nine; a Canadian soldier was also killed. Those convicted of mutiny and striking were given one or two years' hard labour.

The British executed ten Chinese who were working for them during the war: one was executed for murdering his British commanding officer, the other nine men had killed fellow workers. The sentences were handed down after trials by court-martial – even though the Chinese men were non-combatants and not soldiers.

A Chinese camp in the neighbourhood of Ypres in Belgium

The cap badge of the Chinese Labour Corps

Comfort and Education

The environment in which the men lived and worked in France and Belgium was harsh and dangerous. But they did receive help. For those working with the French, assistance was provided by the Work Study Movement (WSM). For those with the British, support was provided by the Young Men's Christian Association (YMCA).

The Work Study Movement

The WSM was the brainchild of Li Shizeng, the son of a wealthy and respected family in Beijing. Li had left China in 1902 to study biology at the Pasteur Institute in Paris. Six years later he established a soya processing factory in a northwest suburb of Paris, and invited thirty workers from his native village in Hebei to travel to France to work for him. He opened a school to teach his employees French, Chinese and technical subjects, and forbade them from smoking, drinking or gambling. It was

Li's belief that a blend of labour and study would turn his workers into informed and independent citizens.

In 1905, Li had joined the Tong Meng Hui, the forerunner of the Kuomintang, the revolutionary party that aimed to overthrow the Qing dynasty. An intellectual and entrepreneur, Li praised France as a 'model republic' from which China should learn. Key to this belief was that Chinese should be sent to the West to learn and be educated in science, social progress and modern industry.

After the success of the Xinhai Revolution in October 1911, a new Republican government took office in China; its Minister of Education was Cai Yuanpei, a pioneer in the reform of culture and education, and a friend of Li. With Cai's support, Li set up the WSM, with the aim to educate Chinese workers and students, to enable each to learn about the other and cure them of their traditional curses – drinking, gambling and smoking opium. In February 1912, Li and four associates, including Cai, established the Association for Frugal Study in France. The association ran preparatory schools in Beijing and Chengdu, and organised the placement of students in schools in France. In 1912 and 1913, Li's organisation sponsored 120 young Chinese to travel to France.

The arrival of the workers during World War One gave Li and his associates a golden opportunity to implement their ideas on a grand scale. They pressed the government to send the workers so they could learn new skills and social customs in Europe, which they could then take home to improve China. 'The Chinese workers in France will form the nucleus of a future trained working class, who will contribute to the spreading of industrial know how on their return to China', Li was quoted as saying in 1917. 'Having been exposed to European civilisation, they can help to reform society and eliminate undesirable habits.'

In June 1916, with the help of Cai and prominent French citizens, Li set up the Sino-French Education Society to develop cooperation and cultural ties between the two countries and help the organisation of the workers during their time in France. Also that year, aided by an annual subsidy of 10 000 francs from the government, the society set up a School for Chinese Workers in Paris, which taught Chinese, French, science, mathematics, culture and public organisation. One of the school's objectives was to train the best-educated workers to act as interpreters and teachers for the other labourers. The first students were twenty-four Chinese who had already been living in France for some time.

The WSM organised evening classes for the workers and established the *Chinese Workers Magazine*, which ran for three and a half years. Written in vernacular language, rather than the centuries-old formal literary style that was used to write Chinese, the magazine was easy to read and achieved a wide readership among the workers, its circulation reaching a peak of 30000 readers by 1918. In one camp in Les Vosges, 5 per cent could read the magazine in May 1917; a year later, readership had grown to 30 per cent.

The magazine stressed the importance of education and learning Western ways, and published news about the workers, the war, China and the world. A list of words in English, French and Chinese was included in the back pages of each issue. The first issue contained a map of Europe, showing the different belligerents and blaming Germany for starting the war: 'This country wants the whole world to belong to it. It is the enemy of humanity.'

For many workers, the magazine was their most important source of information about the outside world; they could also see how other workers were being treated. One issue reported a strike by German workers in the country's biggest munitions factory and the implementation of rationing there. Another described how sixteen Chinese workers in a factory in Bourges had been sent home for theft, gambling and brawling. In another, it was reported that 900 Chinese workers in Vonges, in eastern France, were raising pigs and planting vegetables during their free time. A Chinese worker living in Paris was quoted as saying: 'I have come to France not only because the wages are higher than at home but also for its political ideas. France is a model republic where trade unions defend the interests of the workers. I want to gain experiences, knowledge and general education which will be useful to me after my return to China.'

The *Chinese Workers Magazine* promoted the ideals of WSM – education, mutual assistance, uprightness and a frugal life. It gave guidance on how to behave in France: dress properly and wear a hat when you go out; do not touch anything when you visit a museum; do not talk loudly in a cinema or theatre after the show has begun; walk on the pavement, not the street, and do not pick up what others have dropped. One issue in 1917 advised that the men should not quarrel or fight over small matters; they should not lend money to friends except in emergencies; they should not smoke, drink or gamble; and they should not waste money. On Sundays, the magazine suggested, it was possible to do many things, such as learn French, read or visit museums, activities that would 'allow us to learn and make new friends'. The aim was to stop the habits that many work-ers brought with them from the countryside – talking in a loud voice, spitting, quarrelling noisily and gambling – which made them unpopular with Europeans. One issue published a letter from the Chinese ambassador in France to the workers: 'It is illegal to stop work. Gambling is banned in China as it is abroad. It is unacceptable to fight each other and you must be punctual for work,' he said.

Li Shizeng was critical of the Huimin Company, and the WSM became directly involved in the recruitment of workers. In an article published in his magazine in 1917, Li wrote that Huimin's only motive was profit, that it treated workers like slaves and did not have a proper selection process. He alleged that the company recruited hoodlums who gambled and visited prostitutes in France, creating a bad image among French people.

In 1916, the WSM sent a representative to Yunnan and Guangxi to recruit workers itself and succeeded in signing up between 2500 and 5000 men. The WSM's contracts differed from those given to Huimin applicants. Along with promising to pay the same wages as French workers received, the employer also promised to educate the Chinese employees; in exchange, they must have no bad habits.

The Young Men's Christian Association

On the British side, the YMCA organised a large number of Chinese-speaking missionaries and other volunteers to provide education, recreation and spiritual comfort. The nature of the two organisations, however, was different. The YMCA was an initiative of Western Christian churches, and had a proselytising objective. The WSM was Chinese, organised with the support of the French government, and had social and political – but not religious – objectives.

According to the booklet 'YMCA with the Chinese Labour Corps in France', published in 1919, 'on the arrival of the first contingent of the CLC in France, steps were taken by the British National Council of the YMCA to provide social, recreational and educational work among them. To begin with, there were difficulties. Military officers were suspicious of Chinese-speaking workers coming into camp and having sympathetic relations with the labourers to the prejudice of discipline. For this reason, the early offers of the YMCA were rejected.' Gradually, however, the YMCA received the support of Colonel Fairfax and other officers, due to favourable reports of the Chinese volunteers' activities, and although formal permission was still to be obtained, centres were opened at Calais, Dunkirk, Boulogne, Étaples, Dieppe, Le Havre and Abbeville. The British Army formally invited the YMCA to assist in February 1918.

The YMCA volunteers arranged talks, parties and entertainment, including films, as an alternative to gambling, which had terrible and sometimes fatal consequences. The YMCA volunteers numbered 641 men and women in early 1917, rising to 1024 men and 735 women in February 1919. Only a few could speak Chinese. By the end of 1918, more than eighty centres had been established, providing services for more than 100 of the 194 companies working for the CLC.

The YMCA was also active in helping men working for the French; by 1919, it had set up thirty-eight centres serving more than 70 per cent of those working with the French. The International Committee had sixty-one secretaries in the British area, all Chinese-speaking: thirty-nine were Chinese and twenty-two British or American. Within the French area, there were twenty-one Chinese and fourteen Chinese-speaking Americans.

The typical YMCA centre had a large central room and canteen counter. The men could come here after work to drink tea, play games, watch films, hear lectures and attend educational classes, religious services and Bible classes. Sports included soccer, volleyball, checkers, basketball, ping-pong and boxing. There was also drama, and traditional music and opera; theatrical shows – censored, of course – were very popular.

The men worked seven days a week for the British, with their only break on traditional Chinese holidays, which they celebrated by decorating their huts, making paper lanterns, dining on special meals and staging shows and traditional operas. They also gave demonstrations of tai chi and other martial arts, and played the musical instruments they had brought from China.

The staff played an important role liaising between the men and those overseeing them, offering a degree of comfort, care and educational opportunity that they found nowhere else. The workers were treated as individuals, not as a number to be marched to a trench or railway siding and ordered to work without question for the next ten hours. Once a week, the YMCA staff wrote letters home for them, as around 80 per cent of the labourers were illiterate. As many as 50000 letters a month were sent home from France to China, where they were read and re-read by the relatives. The letters were sent in envelopes specially printed by the CLC and were read by military censors to ensure they contained no military secrets.

The most remarkable Chinese member of the YMCA was James Yen (Yan Yang-chu), who was born into a scholarly family in Sichuan. He had studied at a school run by the China Inland Mission and at Hong Kong University, and had graduated from Yale University in 1918. He recalled: 'I found for the first time in my ignorant intellectual life the value of the common people of my own country. What they lacked was education.'

Yen was primarily responsible for the success of the literary classes organised for the workers. He wrote a literary primer that used 1000 basic characters and published a periodical, the *Chinese Workers Weekly*, which used only those characters. He wrote letters for hundreds of workers. One read: 'For the inspection of my elder brother, I have come many 10000 *li* since

I saw you. I am doing well and you need not have anxiety about me. I am earning three francs a day, but, as living is expensive, I cannot send many home yet. As for my quarrelling with you that day in Yaowan, before I left, forget it! I did unworthily. Please take care of our parents and, when I return in three or five years, I will bring enough money to help support them for the rest of their days.'

James Yen was later invited by the education department of the American Expeditionary Force YMCA to travel to Paris to edit a paper for the Chinese workers in France. The paper was founded in January 1919; within three weeks, the paid circulation was 2000, increasing to 15000 at its peak. Like the WSM's *Chinese Workers Magazine*, it was written in vernacular Chinese and contained short items covering world news, including Europe, the United States and China. Because there was no Chinese typeset, Yen wrote the paper in his own calligraphy, which was then lithographed.

The paper's editorials urged the workers not to curse, fight with each other, gamble, steal or visit prostitutes, as the attitude of Westerners towards China and Chinese was based on the workers' behaviour. Its readers were encouraged to submit articles on such topics as their life in France and how to improve education in China.

Both the WSM and YMCA publications were subject to military censorship from the British and French.

Articles dealing with the issues of Shandong and Tibet were often censored and a blank space left on the page.

The missionaries

The YMCA members also included foreign missionaries from China. Among them was my grandfather, Rev. Frederick O'Neill, an Irish Presbyterian minister who had been serving in Faku, Liaoning province, since 1897. In his books and reports, he gave an account of his two years with the CLC.

O'Neill was assigned to the Chinese general hospital in Noyelles-sur-Mer, where he comforted the sick and dying, wrote letters for them, held services and conducted burials. He also managed a facility of the YMCA, which sent men and women to the camps. He and the other missionaries lived together with the workers. They considered the CLC a good opportunity to spread the gospel to young men who had been taken from their home and placed in an environment where they needed spiritual care and comfort.

In one report, he described a bomb attack on a CLC compound: 'At the beginning of the recent great attack, they had not been not many miles behind one of the hottest centres. Bombs scattered a hundred of them working on the roads. They ran. The company was ordered to retire, leaving their kit behind. Stragglers were picked up. No transport was available. By night and day, they trudged along, sleeping anywhere. The nearest they came to danger was when a shell burst on the road, 50 yards ahead. No-one was hurt. An American camp gave them food. On foot, and later by train, they reached the Chinese depot in a week.'

After only a few days, the men were sent to work cutting timber, and they came to hear Frederick preach. 'I praised them for their good behaviour in the battle. They beamed with pleasure. Then, as I talked in a simple way about the true meaning of our religion, about God and Christ and Love, about danger and fear and death and immortality, they listened mouth and eyes. It is almost painful to be watched so intently.'

Just before his return to China in April 1919, O'Neill wrote: 'It can be confidently said that the YMCA has shown the Chinese the spirit of brotherhood. By means of lectures, cinema, literature and religious addresses, thousands of the strangers have received more instruction than ever before in their lives. The outlook of the traveled peasants and artisans will have been widened and the hold of superstition upon them probably lessened. They will have seen Christianity as active service.'

Grandfather and his wife, Annie, left France in mid-May 1919, to return to Liaoning. Along with many British officers and civilians who served with the corps, including another Presbyterian missionary from Manchuria, William Cargin, Rev. O'Neill was decorated by the Chinese government with the Order of Wen Hu (the Striped Tiger) for his work with the CLC.

The newspaper *Huagong Zazhi*, 10 August 1917. The magazine was published twice a month and was well read by intellectuals within the Chinese Labour Corps

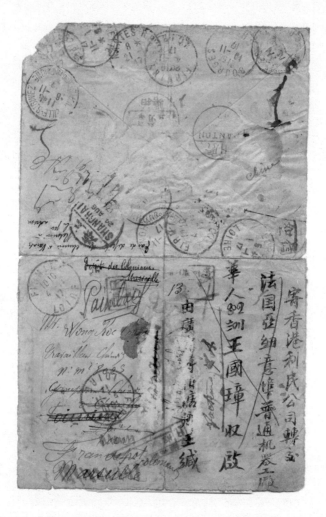

A letter that was never delivered: this letter from 1917 was addressed to Chinese labourer Wang Guozhang. Wang was most probably one of the 543 Chinese labourers that perished when the Athos was torpedoed

War Ends but
the Chinese Remain

When Kaiser Wilhelm II abdicated and the armistice was signed on 11 November 1918, the world erupted in joy. The most terrible war in human history, leaving sixteen million dead and twenty million wounded, had come to an end.

For the soldiers, their long nightmare on the battle-fields was over. They could put down their guns and go home. But the Chinese workers could not return to their homeland; their three- and five-year contracts had not yet expired. In any event, the ships to transport them across the Atlantic were fully booked, carrying tens of thousands of American and Canadian soldiers and civilians; there were no berths for foreign workers.

At the end of the war, more than 200 000 people from British colonies were working for the Allies, including 100 000 Egyptians, 21 000 Indians and 20 000 South Africans. Of the Chinese recruited by the French, about 35 000 remained at war's end; 1200 had been repatriated for reasons of health or indiscipline, and 600 had died because of accidents, disease or disputes. Six months later, 80 000 members of the CLC were still at work, and as late as October 1919, 50 000 remained.

To the Allies, the Chinese men were as valuable after the war as they had been during the conflict. Large areas of northern France and Belgium resembled a lunar landscape, with no building left standing, no roads, railways or telegraph poles; no farmland that could be cultivated. The countryside was covered with trenches and the debris of fifty-two months of fighting – the dead bodies of humans and animals, spent bullets, unexploded shells, barbed wire, rusting vehicles and scrap metal.

The enormous task of reconstruction fell to the French and British armies, each with their own contingent of Chinese. On and behind the front-line, the recovery and removal or destruction of the hundreds of tonnes of ordnance that had been left behind was the responsibility of the Allied army that controlled the area at the time of the armistice. The Chinese men were involved in recovering this materiel for the British Army; it was then sold to local people in the immediate postwar period. However, the workers were not employed in reconstruction work in Britain; the opposition of the trade unions prevented it.

The French moved 70 per cent of their Chinese workforce to the front for salvage and reconstruction work. According to official figures, in the ten French regions where the war had been fought, a total of 11 000 public buildings and 350 000 houses had been destroyed; 2.5 million hectares of land, 62 000 kilometres of roads, 1 858 kilometres of canals and 5 000 kilometres of railways needed to be repaired. Within a month of the armistice, the French government set up the Service des Travaux de Première Urgence (Emergency Works Service) to carry out the most urgent reconstruction work. By 1919, it was employing more than 260 000 people, including 50 000 to 60 000 French, 200 000 prisoners of war and colonial workers, and 25 000 Chinese.

The Chinese were employed to indicate the presence of unexploded shells – which French specialists would later detonate – remove barbed wire and the carcasses of animals, fill the trenches, rework the soil and rebuild homes. They also dug ditches to return water to the farmland so agricultural production could be resumed as soon as possible, as those living behind what had been the German lines were close to starvation. Others worked on farms or in factories, and 230 men were sent to work in the mines.

Clearing ammunition, some of it live, was a difficult

and dangerous job. The men were given no specialised training, and some workers died or were injured. Another thankless job was the collection and burial of dead soldiers, a task that was especially difficult for the Chinese, who believed that touching a corpse brought bad luck.

Relations sour

As the months passed, relations deteriorated between the Chinese and the local inhabitants, who had rushed home from exile in other parts of France, eager to recover their homes and prevent others from looting or moving in. They wanted to resume normal life as soon as possible and resented the presence of so many foreigners. But the times were anything but normal; they were anarchic. The pillars of civilian government, including the police, were not in place; public services were poor, if they existed at all. Some Chinese took advantage of this anarchy to break into houses and steal the contents; sometimes they demanded money from the residents or attacked them. The local media reported such cases in great detail. Another complaint against the Chinese was their habit of blowing up fireworks and munitions close to houses, terrifying those inside.

For their part, the workers had their own grievances. They too wanted to go home at the end of the war, but they now found themselves in accommodation that was often worse than the camps or barracks they'd inhabited during the conflict. They were housed in barns or partly destroyed buildings, former army camps or leaking tents with mud floors. When they had no fuel for heating or cooking, they stole wood from railway lines or coal from nearby rail depots. The support network in place during the war – such as the YMCA centres – was removed, the staff sent home, and the men had limited medical care. The tight discipline under which they had worked during the war loosened, and weapons were everywhere for the taking.

Disputes escalated as the men met other Chinese workers and compared pay and conditions. At the end of the summer of 1919, a group of 400 to 500 workers marched towards the town of Soissons to demand the pay not given to them for a month and to protest against violence inflicted against one of their number. Armed soldiers were put in position on the outskirts of the town with orders to open fire. Fortunately, an army colonel who spoke Mandarin was found; he stepped forward, listened to the grievances of the workers and prevented a massacre.

It was the same story in the rural region of Westhoek in western Flanders, also devastated by the fighting. Public opinion had been favourable to the presence of the Chinese workers during the war. On the occasion of the Chinese New Year, on 11 February 1918, the inhabitants of the city of Poperinghe had celebrated the event together with the Chinese. But the situation changed after the armistice, as it did in the Pas-de-Calais. Residents returned after months in exile to find their homes and farms in ruins, and soldiers and workers from fifty-five different cultures ensconced there, the most foreign and bizarre being the Chinese.

Residents and the local media reported crimes committed by the Chinese, including the murder of a local man named Jules Bailleul at his home on the night of 9 May 1919. 'More and more, the region is less secure because of all kinds of strange things – looting at the front and especially the Chinese,' wrote Bailleul's parish priest, Achiel Van Walleghem, in his journal. 'The British officers who were less numerous had no more authority over these men. They escaped from their camp and wandered armed with guns and grenades which they found easily.'

Between April and August 1919, senators from western Flanders speaking in the Belgian Parliament described a list of crimes committed by the Chinese, and demanded the rapid withdrawal of 'all colonial troops'. In reply, the Minister of War, Fulgence Masson, said on 17 June that the 12 000 Chinese workers in western Flanders were doing a useful and dangerous job in rehabilitating the battlefields: 'If they were withdrawn immediately, this task would fall to the Belgians. So it would be more advantageous for Belgium to let them finish their work.'

Masson also commented that the number of crimes and offences committed by the Chinese had been exaggerated by the press and public opinion. In this atmosphere of fear and insecurity, it was easy to invoke the 'yellow peril', since the Chinese were considered the 'most strange' of the foreign workers. All the government could do, Masson said, was to ask the British Army to increase the number of officers attached to the CLC and improve discipline; for example, ordering the men to stay within a radius of 200 to 300 metres around their camps.

The British and French governments may have wished to repatriate the Chinese for the sake of social peace and to please public opinion, but they could not – the work the labourers were carrying out was too essential, and it involved tasks that their own nationals did not want to perform. On 31 August 1919, a French Army captain named Leboeuf reported to his superiors that his company of Chinese had filled in 23 523 square metres of trenches, averaging 10.5 square metres per worker per day: 'If the Chinese workers are under the control of conscientious civilians, three or four good supervisors (gangers) and tightly controlled by their military commander, they can achieve good results, whatever people in the liberated areas say.'

In August 1919, a letter by General Nollet, commander of the First Army Corps, was published in several newspapers in northern France, stating that 'your desire to see all the Chinese leave France cannot be realised without enormous damage to the reconstruction of the liberated areas. The workers provide a clearing work that is very effective and so important that they cannot be replaced by civil and military (French) workers.'

The men finally return home

As the work was eventually completed, so the men were sent home. They did not return empty-handed. A report by the Chinese Embassy in London put the volume of savings held by the workers in French banks on 26 May 1919 at 51 million francs; an average of 800 francs was saved after three years, 1300 francs after five. This sum did not include the money that the men had already sent home to their families in China.

By September 1920, Britain had repatriated all of its approximately 94400 Chinese workers, of whom seventy-three died during the return journey. No Chinese labourers working for Britain were permitted to remain in Europe. Before being sent home, some 191 Chinese from the CLC had served with the Slavo-British Legion in northern Russia, as part of the 255500 foreign troops fighting in Russia from 1918 to 1920 on behalf of the pro-tsar White Russians against the Bolsheviks.

France had repatriated its workers by the end of 1922, the Chinese being the last contingent of foreign workers to leave. Three thousand chose to stay behind.

The vast majority of workers returned, as they had come, via Canada, where they were treated with the same strict control and popular indifference they had encountered on their outward journey. While Canadian soldiers returning from the front were greeted as heroes with welcoming parties, bunting and smiling girls, the Chinese were ignored.

On 17 February 1920, the Halifax *Herald* published an article entitled 'Great events which pass unnoticed'. It noted that 'when all things are seen in their proper perspective, the place accorded to the Chinese labor units will be equal to that of the highest and the best . . . the largest camps of the Chinese on the Canadian front were subjected daily to long-range shelling and in the moonless nights they were regularly bombed . . . They were road-builders and were invaluable in maintaining the ration-route; they furnished carrying parties in the sectors where transportation was poor, and in a thousand other ways they carried out work that was in every respect as essential towards winning the war as the barrage, [and] the over-the-top.'

Separate in death, as in life

Almost all the Chinese who served with the British took home a bronze war medal engraved with the profile of King George V and their personal multi-digit military number. It was the same as the medal given to every member of the British armed forces – except it was of bronze, not silver.

In addition, certain members of the CLC received awards for devotion to duty, including the Meritorious Service Medal. One went to Wang Yushao, number 15333, of the 59th company of the CLC. His citation read:

'Near Marcoing (near Cambrai) on June 9, 1919, he observed a fire on an ammunition dump close to a collecting station. On his own initiative, he rushed to the dump with two buckets of water which he threw on the fire and then seized a burning British "P" bomb [apparently the cause of the outbreak] and hurled it to a safe distance from the dump. He then continued to extinguish the burning dump which had spread to the surrounding grass in which rifle grenades and German shells were lying. By his initiative, resource and disregard of personal safety, this labourer averted what might have been a serious explosion.'

There were many other examples of acts of heroism to prevent explosions and accidents, and save others under enemy fire – some of them occurring in combat situations, showing how the spirit, if not the letter, of the men's contract had been broken. The only workers who did not receive medals were those who had been court-martialled.

The last sixty members of the CLC remaining in France were given a sombre task – carving the names on the tombstones of the dead workers. In France and Belgium, there are 2000 CLC graves. The men died as a result of bombing, shelling and gassing; from the unexploded ordnance they were clearing after the war; and from accidents and disease, including tuberculosis and the deadly Spanish influenza, which killed more than 400000 people in France. The preference of the Chinese was that their bodies should be shipped home for burial, but this was impossible in the conditions of war and postwar. Four cemeteries were set aside for the Chinese workers; the remainder lie buried in forty military cemeteries in France and Belgium, in plots set apart from the Commonwealth graves. The bodies of the British officers and NCOs of the CLC were buried among the other Commonwealth dead. In death as in life, the Chinese were treated differently.

The British Army built a beautiful cemetery at Noyelles-sur-Mer, close to the CLC headquarters and hospital. Each funeral was attended by the medical officer of the day and the coffin was covered by the Union Jack and carried by other patients.

Today, the cemetery remains the main site to remember the Chinese workers. On the date of the Qing Ming festival, representatives of the Chinese Embassy, the Chinese community in France and the French Army have in recent years gathered to lay wreaths in memorial at the site. The cemetery is guarded by two stone lions, gifts from China, and contains 842 gravestones, each engraved with one of four proverbs inscribed in Chinese characters: 'faithful unto death', 'a good reputation endures forever', 'a noble duty bravely done' and 'though dead, he still lives'. Maintained by the Commonwealth War Graves Commission, each headstone bears the name of the corps, the man's number, the date of his death in English, and his name and native province in Chinese. Those who were court-martialled are also buried here.

Estimates vary about the ultimate death toll, with some publications placing the figure as high as 10 000. The most recent research suggests that the figure was around 3 000. Due to the many different causes of death in wartime, a precise number is hard to calculate. No-one kept an exact record.

A Chinese labourer amidst the destroyed graves in the churchyard of the village of Dikkebus near Ypres

The bronze British War Medal that was issued to all members of the Chinese Labour Corps who had served with the British Army in the First World War

Betrayal at Versailles

After the armistice, anticipation in China was high. There were triumphant parades in Beijing; an excited crowd demolished a memorial that the Qing had been forced to raise in honour of the Germans killed by the Boxers. For the first time, China was a member of an international alliance that had won a major military conflict. Also for the first time, China would sit at the top table of international powers. Liang Shiyi's calculation in the early days of the war had proved accurate; he had forecast a victory of the Allied powers and persuaded two nations to accept large contingents of workers. They had served with bravery and perseverance, and made an important contribution to the victory.

The Foreign Ministry sent a delegation of sixty-two officials to attend the conference that would decide the peace. It opened on 18 January 1919 in the enormous Palace of Versailles, southwest of Paris, attended by delegations from twenty-six countries. One of the largest palaces in the world, Versailles was one of the few structures to rival the Forbidden City in Beijing. Both buildings were symbols of absolute monarchy, intended to awe those who enter and make them realise their own unimportance, a message that was perhaps ignored by the Chinese delegates who imagined a new world of democracy and equality.

China's demands were modest for a conference that redrew the map of the world in a way never done before in history. It demanded that Germany's concessions in Shandong be returned to Chinese control. It also demanded an end to colonial institutions in the country – extra-territoriality and foreign concessions where foreign countries could station troops. These demands were in accord with the fourteen points proclaimed by US President Woodrow Wilson in January 1918, which set out his aims for the postwar world.

But when Foreign Minister Lu Zhengxiang and his colleagues arrived at the ornate palace, they were in for a nasty shock. Their five negotiators had been reserved just two chairs, opposite their five Japanese counterparts, each of whom had his own seat. For China, Japan was a greater enemy than Germany or the Ottoman Empire. They then learned that Article 156 of the treaty gave Germany's interests in Shandong to Japan. They also discovered the dishonesty of their own government, which had not briefed them on two secret agreements it had signed with Japan, giving it political and economic rights in Shandong.

The Japanese delegation argued that, as an ally of Britain, it had entered the war in August 1914 and helped its allies during the war. In February 1915, marines from its ships based in Singapore had helped suppress a mutiny by Indian troops against the British government. In 1917, at London's request, it sent a Second Special Squadron of seventeen ships to Malta, from where they carried out escort duties for troop transports and anti-submarine operations. They made 348 sorties from Malta, escorting 788 shops with 700 000 soldiers, greatly helping the war effort. They rescued 7 075 people from damaged and sinking ships, and lost sixty-eight dead and suffered heavy damage to the destroyer *Sakaki*, after it was torpedoed by an Austrian submarine. In exchange for this naval assistance, Britain, France and Italy had signed secret treaties of support for Japan's claims to German concessions in Shandong after the war.

In contrast, China had not entered the war until August 1917, and had sent no fighting forces. British Foreign Secretary Arthur Balfour said that China's contribution during the war had involved neither 'the expenditure of a single shilling nor the loss of a single life' – completely ignoring the contribution of the workers. The Chinese soon discovered that the negotiations had little to do with Wilson's high-sounding fourteen points and everything to do with the interests of the victors.

On 28 January 1919, Wellington Koo, spokesman for the Chinese delegation, made a passionate speech about Shandong; he was at that time ignorant of the agreements his government had signed with Japan. He described Shandong as the 'cradle of Chinese civilisation', the birthplace of Confucius and Mencius. China could no more give it up than Christians could abandon Jerusalem. If Japan continued its lease of the Shandong territory, it would provide it with a strategic gateway to all of north China.

Koo's words moved many of the delegates, but President Wilson and his European allies believed that, in accordance with international law and treaties, Japan should receive all of Germany's rights in Shandong. Outraged, the Chinese delegation left the negotiations and sent news of the decision to their masters in Beijing. It provoked an uproar. The government was bombarded by petitions and protests, including those from Chinese students and workers in France, who were able to follow the deliberations more closely than their compatriots at home. Especially bitter were the workers, who believed that the return of the Shandong rights was the main reason their government had sent them to assist in the war effort.

The deadline for signing the treaty was 28 June. The government in Beijing ordered the delegation to return to Versailles to sign the agreement, but Chinese students and workers in Paris surrounded the Chinese officials' hotel and prevented them from attending the signing ceremony.

The final treaty was signed by twenty-six of the twenty-seven victorious powers – but not China. It declared the end of its war with Germany in September 1919 and signed a separate treaty with Germany in 1921.

During the Washington Naval Conference of 1922, the United States mediated the dispute and the sovereignty of Shandong was returned to China on 4 February that year, with Japanese residents living in the region given special rights.

Liang Shiyi's bet to send the workers had won him a place at the victors' table, but none of the spoils. Kang You-wei's prophecy had proved to be correct: 'There is no such thing as an army of righteousness which will come to the assistance of weak nations.'

China's place in the Victory Parade

China's rightful place among the victors was underlined by its presence in a giant victory parade that wove its way through the streets of London on Saturday 19 July 1919. A group of seven officers on horseback, in full dress uniform and carrying the national flag, were among the 15 000 soldiers from eighteen nations that took part.

The parade was the largest ever held in London, the capital of a global empire that had seen many such spectacles, and was the highlight of four days of events held to celebrate Britain's victory in the most terrible war in history. Of the eighteen nations represented, only three were Asian – China, Japan and India, then a British colony.

At the request of Prime Minister David Lloyd George, architect Edwin Lutyens had designed the Cenotaph – meaning 'empty tomb' in Greek – as a monument to those killed or wounded. In less than two weeks, he'd crafted the wood and plaster neoclassical design that was unveiled that morning in Whitehall. Within hours, onlookers had piled wreaths of flowers around its base. A permanent monument, cast in Portland Stone, was unveiled at the same spot in 1920 and has been the site of a service of remembrance on the Sunday closest to Armistice Day, 11 November, ever since.

The parade's largest contingents were provided by Britain and France, the two countries most responsible for the victory. The Chinese officers were led by Lieutenant-General Tang Zaili. A native of Shanghai, he had been sent to Paris to lead the China Expeditionary Force intended to be sent to France. He set up his headquarters in the city, but the taskforce never left China.

The symbolism of China's participation in the parade was greater than the small number of soldiers that took part. It was the first time a Chinese contingent had been included in an international military parade. On that day, London was the centre of the world. Global media had gathered to record the event, and many reported the Chinese presence as something new and striking. A large photograph of the seven officers appeared in the *Illustrated London News*.

Life for the Returnees

The Chinese workers were changed by their experience in Europe, especially those who had taken the opportunity to educate themselves. Many learnt to read and obtained an understanding of a wider world that would have been impossible if they had stayed labouring on the farm in the Shandong countryside or unloading sacks of rice at the port of Tianjin.

In 2009, Zhang Yan, a researcher in the history department of the University of Shandong, interviewed the descendants of sixty-five returnees, largely in the Zhoucun district of Zibo city, Shandong. He discovered that the workers did not fulfil the hopes of intellectuals such as Li Shizeng, who hoped they would act as a force for change in Chinese society. The men returned to a rural and deeply traditional society, which was not at all ready to accept change. Zhang found that their impact was insignificant, due to the men's social status and the restrictions of society and of the era.

'Overall, the lot of the returnees was tragic,' Zhang found. 'This was due to the cruel nature of Chinese society and the political situation, and the passive treatment they received from the Chinese, British and French governments. After the war, the British and French governments considered them a burden they wanted to dispose of as soon as possible; the interests of many returnees, especially those who died or were disabled, were not properly compensated for. In addition, the Beijing government did not protect and make provision for them nor did it make use of the rich knowledge and experience they had built up.' Plans to use the men in industry, construction and other fields came to nothing. Nor did they play a role in efforts to found trade unions or make changes in society.

The men brought with them mementoes from Europe that delighted and amazed their family and neighbours; items such as Swiss watches, pictures of French scenery, military uniforms, sound recorders, leather shoes and machines that played short films. The money they had earned with such difficulty was soon spent: custom demanded that it be shared with brothers, sisters, cousins and heads of the family.

Zhu Wenzeng, for example, had eight brothers and sisters with whom he had to share his earnings. Another returnee, Li Fenglong, had six brothers and sisters. 'Although they both brought back a considerable sum, they quickly fell back into the same poverty in which they had lived before. Li Baogui was so angry that his earnings were being shared among his family that he ran away,' wrote Zhang Yan in his report. Only a very small number of returnees set up factories or went into business. The vast majority resumed their previous occupation as farmers; some lost all their savings on gambling.

Of the sixty-five returnees studied by Zhang, ten never married because they were too poor or disabled. Two had no home of their own and resorted to living in a temple. Wu Lizhong was injured during his service and totally disabled; for the rest of his life, he depended on his younger brother. He Licai was the object of class struggle during the Cultural Revolution because he had left the country. He took his own life.

But others were inspired by what they had seen in France, and initiated such changes as introducing water pumps and tractors to their farms. One of the workers, Sun Gan, influenced by rural education in France, established the first rural school for girls in Zibo. Another, Li Rongkun, removed the binding from the feet of his three daughters and sent them to school.

Li Ma, a French scholar of Chinese origin who edited a major book on the workers, wrote that in the summer of 2010 she met the descendants of thirty-five families of the workers from the cities of Zibo, Zhoucun and

Weihai in Shandong. 'I met a grandfather of eighty-five whose uncle returned from France with agricultural tools. He showed them to me. He explained to me that the workers had great difficulty in speaking of their experiences in the war. They were traumatised; they spoke of the planes and the bombardments. According to the contract, they should not have taken part in combat or be on the front-line. But that changed and they found themselves on the battlefield.' They lived off the money they had earned in France; when it ran out, they were penniless and once again became farmers in Shandong. Some returned with syphilis, contracted from French prostitutes close to the front. 'Many workers returned home with French wives, often their second wives. They were not accepted by the families at home. Many had to go back to France with the aid of the consul.'

Some workers returned to China having lost their sight or been seriously injured. The contract with the CLC provided for compensation of only 75 dollars, which became an issue between the Chinese and British governments. In late 1918, the British War Office agreed to more generous terms, with eighteen months' pay given to the family of a man who died during service. It ruled out paying pensions, however, saying it could not properly administer the payments to people in China.

Working with a Belgian scholar, Philip Vanhaele-meersch, Zhang Yan co-authored a report on thirteen workers killed in a German air raid on their camp in Poperinghe, Belgium, on 15 November 1917. The men were buried in a nearby village, and their remains were later taken to a cemetery in Bailleul, northern France. The two authors discovered that the news of the workers' deaths had never been sent to their families in Shandong. They passed the results of their research on to the relatives, who were surprised and moved, relieved that they were able to close this chapter of their family history.

On 29 May 2010, Poperinghe held a memorial service for the thirteen workers, attended by the city's mayor and the Chinese acting ambassador to Belgium, Chen Xiaoming. A commemorative plaque was unveiled, and the acting ambassador captured the mood well when he said: 'Today's event not only affirms the spirits of the dead but also gives comfort to their descendants. It encourages the peoples of the two countries to work together.'

Intellectual impact

The impact was greater on the Chinese intellectuals who engaged with the workers. Before the war, the two groups lived in separate universes. The intellectual pursued his studies in China and abroad, and, armed with his diplomas and connections, went on to a career in the government, a university or a company. He had no desire or need to meet the millions of farmers and workers who made up the vast majority of his countrymen. Likewise, a Shandong farmer or Tianjin port worker would have no occasion or opportunity to meet the men with expensive ties and pin-striped suits who spoke a refined Chinese most of them could not understand. The war in France threw them together.

Men such as the YMCA's James Yen, intellectual Lin Yu-tang and student Jiang Ting-fu saw the workers not as illiterate peasants but as their compatriots who were struggling to survive in the middle of a war in a foreign country and needed their help. At their service centres, they wrote letters, provided literacy classes, and hosted music performances and lectures to enable the men to learn about the world. They were astonished at how quickly the workers learnt, and realised that it was only the lack of literacy that blocked their potential. Thanks to their assistance, many workers were able to read by the time they returned home.

These members of China's elite were changed by their experience. Lin Yu-tang cut short his doctorate studies at Harvard to volunteer with the workers. He went on to become one of the most famous Chinese authors and intellectuals of the twentieth century.

James Yen commented: 'I had never associated with labourers before the war . . . we of the student class felt ourselves altogether apart from them. But there in

France I had the privilege of associating with them daily and knowing them intimately. I found that these men were just as good as I. The only difference between us was that I had had advantages and they had not.'

With his excellent academic qualifications, Yen could have chosen to pursue a good career in government, academia or business in China. Instead, in 1923, he established the National Association for Mass Education in China; it spread to thousands of villages in every province of the country. He spent the rest of his life working in mass education, in China, the Philippines and other countries, and established the Internal Institute of Rural Reconstruction.

Yen was a strong personality and a charismatic speaker, but he felt that the workers taught him more than he taught them. In 1943, he was chosen as one of the ten most influential men in the world, together with Henry Ford and Albert Einstein.

Staying in France

An estimated 3000 Chinese workers chose to remain in France after the war, having married French wives or signed a work contract with a new employer.

The war had killed 1.7 million French people, nearly all the men of marriageable age. One-third of the male population aged between thirteen and thirty had died; for those aged fifteen to forty-nine, the figure was 13.3 per cent. The death toll was equivalent to more than 4 per cent of the population, the greatest loss suffered by the combatant nations; more than four million were wounded. In a country with a population of only forty million, these statistics were alarming, raising fears that the nation might disappear. To ensure the future of France, some even proposed allowing a man to have several wives.

Most of the Chinese labourers met their wives in the factories where they worked building machinery, tanks or other weapons. The most fortunate workers were the early arrivals who worked in the factories and were not posted near the front – they enjoyed the same holidays as French workers and were able to mix with the local people. The Chinese were aged between eighteen and forty, and were in good health, hardworking and efficient. They saved their money, rather than spending it in the bars and restaurants.

Jiang Ting-fu, an American-educated student who ran a Chinese service centre in Paris, commented that the French had less prejudice than the British and enjoyed better relations with the workers, eating together and sharing jokes and stories. He cited the example of a French woman who came to see him at his centre, and told him that she wished to marry a Chinese named Yang, and was even prepared to travel to China with him. 'Unlike many French men, he does not drink and has never beaten me up. If I found a French man, he might be alcoholic, spend all our money on wine and beat me up frequently. If I do not marry Mr Yang, I will have no chance to marry at all,' she said.

The French government did not encourage this trend, and was especially opposed to the idea of couples leaving the country after their marriage. French women should marry the French men who were returning from military service abroad. The government decided to ban women from sailing on the boats that were taking the men home to China. One worker smuggled his wife on board in a blanket, but she was discovered and taken back to shore. He never saw her again.

However, if the couple stayed in France and brought up their children there, the government was more favourable. According to a report by Captain Brissaud Desmaillet to the Ministry of War in June 1925, seventy Chinese workers married French women. Among them was Zhang Chang-song, who left for France in June 1917, worked for eight months on the docks moving cargo and was later employed burying corpses. He was then transferred to a machinery plant, where he met his future wife, Louise, a cleaner in the factory. They married in 1921, with the certificate issued by the Chinese Embassy in Paris.

A law of 1801 stated that a French woman who married a foreigner lost her French nationality. In the aftermath of the war, the French government reversed this policy, in an attempt to offset the huge losses in population. Between 1914 and 1927, around 120000 French women had married foreigners – losing their citizenship; 60000 foreign women who married French men had gained it. The modification allowed women like Louise to regain her French nationality, and she and her husband had a second, civil wedding ceremony. When Zhang converted to Catholicism, they organised a third ceremony in a church. Zhang worked in a coal mine for thirty-two years, without an accident. The couple were happily married for more than sixty years and had thirteen children, who spoke very little Chinese.

The most famous Chinese immigrant was Zhu Guisheng, who signed a five-year contract in 1916. He arrived in France after an exhausting voyage of five months, and lived in three different camps during the war. In 1922, Zhu married a French woman and obtained French citizenship. The couple settled in the western port city of La Rochelle, and had one son and two daughters. Zhu worked as a crane driver, docker and electrician, and he served with distinction in the French Army during World War Two. He became a well-known citizen, visited by the mayor on his birthday. When Zhu died in 2002, at the age of 106, the last surviving Chinese worker from World War One, the city's mayor praised him as a model of integration into

French society and the pride of the citizens of La Rochelle.

One of Zhu's neighbours was Liu Desheng, who had also worked at the port of La Rochelle during the war and fallen in love with a local girl. On three occasions he was sent to Marseilles for repatriation to China; he escaped each time, and was captured and returned to Marseilles twice. Finally, he was able to marry his sweetheart, and the couple raised fifteen children during their long marriage.

In an interview with a French scholar, one of their daughters noted that her mother's family had not opposed the marriage. Her grandmother told her: 'At least, Mr Liu will not drink and beat her.' After their marriage, Liu gave his salary to his wife and allowed her to continue working, freedoms that were rare among married women in France at that time. He cultivated a vegetable garden and cooked Chinese dishes for himself, but he did not speak Chinese to his children and never spoke about China or his life in the camps during the war. He cut all links with his original family in China.

One of the men who left on the same ship as Zhu Guisheng was Bi Cui-de; the two men came from the same village in Shandong. Bi was aged twenty, and left a wife and one-year-old son behind. He died on 9 September 1919 when the ammunition he was carrying exploded. All his family in Shandong received was his war medal and the compensation payment. He lies buried in a grave identified by the number 97237.

Belated recognition

Some workers stayed in the villages in the Somme but most went to live in the area around Gare de Lyon in Paris's 13th arrondissement. They worked in industry, especially in the Louis Renault car factory in Boulogne-Bilancourt and the Panhard and Levassor factories.

Some of the men came from Qingtian, outside Wenzhou, Zhejiang province. One was Ye Qingyuan, a native of Qingtian who volunteered at the end of 1917. 'My home village was a poor mountain village, a disaster for heaven and man alike, where you could not make a living,' he wrote in his diary. 'When Germany surrendered in November 1918, the government gave us a bonus. With my cousin, I opened a restaurant near the Gare de Lyon in Paris. The French were very curious and wanted to sample Chinese food. Within six months, we were run off our feet.'

By the end of 1920, Ye had enough money to return home, marry a local girl and return to Paris with three of his brothers. They opened restaurants and shops that sold groceries and carved stone from Qingtian. When Ye retired in 1985, he returned, finally, to live in his ancestral village in China.

The early arrivals kept a low profile in Paris and, eager to integrate, emphasised their Frenchness. Joining this community in the 1920s were Deng Xiaoping and Zhou Enlai, future leaders of the Communist revolution, who went to France under a work-study program.

As the years passed, the history and contribution of the workers was forgotten, especially among the French population, and it was not acknowledged by the government. It was not until November 1988 that a modest bronze plaque was erected on the wall of a Paris building belonging to SNCF, the state railway company, to commemorate its Chinese workers. Seventy years after the end of the war, this was the first official acknowledgement. A year later, two of the Chinese workers who were still alive received the French Légion d'Honneur.

In 1922, during the Qing Ming festival, nearly 800 people, French and Chinese, took part in the first large-scale memorial event; they included thirty representatives of the French Army and veterans' organisations. In November 2008, a monument was unveiled in a park in the 13th arrondissement, now the Chinatown of Paris. It reads, in French and Chinese: 'In memory of Chinese workers and fighters who died for France in the Great War'.

Gerard Tchang, whose father arrived in France in 1917 from Huaian in Jiangsu, is bitter about this belated recognition. 'Now in France no-one knows of this history. I saw an exhibition of the war at the City Hall of Paris and there was no mention of the Chinese. This history has been completely forgotten. Today, people receive medals who did much less than my father. Is it because he was Chinese?'

Philippe Liang, now in his eighties, is a native of Xiamen who moved to Vietnam and then France. 'When I arrived in France in the 1940s, there was racism against Chinese but not now, when it is directed against blacks and Arabs. The status of Chinese is rising. Some have very substantial businesses.'

Today, the Chinese community in France has grown to more than half a million. Unlike the early arrivals, they have a confidence and self-belief that comes from economic success, integration into mainstream society and the growth and prosperity of their homeland. The second and third generations have done well, better than many of the immigrants from France's former colonies in Africa.

Each year, on the Qing Ming festival, members of the Chinese community gather to leave wreaths at the Chinatown monument, at the SNCF plaque and at the cemeteries in northern France where the Chinese workers are buried.

The headstone of a Chinese labourer at Lijssenthoek Military Cemetery, Poperinge, Belgium

Conclusion

The workers' participation in the most catastrophic war in history brought no benefit to China. They were sent to France in the expectation that China would be rewarded for its participation, but the victorious powers gave China no reduction in the payment of the Boxer Indemnity. Nor did they listen to Beijing's demands for an end to colonial privileges. In 1919, a Chinese policeman in Shanghai could not arrest a drunk Britain or Frenchman beating up a rickshaw driver any more than he could in 1913. The leaders of the victorious powers regarded China with the same disdain and prejudice as the vast majority of their citizens regarded the workers.

In fact, the outcome was worse for China after the war. The distant imperial power of Germany was replaced in Shandong by a closer and more dangerous one – Japan. Wellington Koo's prediction during his speech at Versailles proved to be extremely accurate: just twelve years later, Japan used its occupation of

Shandong to facilitate its takeover of Manchuria, leading to all-out war with China in 1937. Japan's military leaders witnessed China's weakness and corruption during World War One, and the unwillingness of the Western powers to come to its help. Just as the peace settlement at Versailles led to an even more horrific war just twenty years later, the Japanese occupation of Shandong laid the seeds of a terrible war to come.

Diplomatically, China gained nothing from the participation of its workers in the war effort. Nor did the majority of the workers gain from their experience. Some saved money that they could not have earned at home; several thousand made a new life for themselves in France. But many were injured and traumatised by their experiences, which left them unable to resume a normal life at home. The majority returned to the cotton fields and apple orchards to take up the agricultural work they had done before. They would play no role in the political and cultural life of their country.

In taking up the opportunity to travel to Europe, the Chinese workers left the familiar surroundings of home to enter a strange new world, encountering the foreign customs of France and the dangerous reality of wartime.

'All was going well and I was glad I had come, when one night without warning we were suddenly awakened by the sound of a terrific explosion. We

ran outside without delay . . . And nearly every night thereafter our sleep was broken. At the first sound of the gong alarm, we were ordered to the cave shelters. One after another of the fine buildings was destroyed and great holes in the ground could be seen in many places. Many people were killed, even women and children . . . I soon came to dread the clear nights.'

ACKNOWLEDGEMENTS

I would like to thank the many people who made the writing of this book possible.

First is Dominiek Dendooven, researcher at the In Flanders Field Museum in Ypres. He provided most of the excellent photographs for the book and gave his precious time to read and revise the text. In May 2010, his museum and four partners in France and Belgium organised an international conference on the Chinese workers in the First World War. It was the most important academic meeting ever held in Europe on the subject. The papers were published in *Les travailleurs chinois en France dans la Première Guerre mondiale*, edited by Li Ma. This book was an invaluable source of material, with contributions from Belgian, French, British, German, Canadian and Chinese scholars.

Another important source was *Strangers on the Western Front – Chinese Workers in the Great War* by Xu Guoqi, professor of history at the University of Hong Kong;

this is a book rich in detail, the result of years of research.

I must also thank Brian Fawcett, for *The Chinese Labour Corps in France 1917–1921*, and Gregory James who has great knowledge of this subject. Paul French provided excellent photographs, a copy of Daryl Klein's book *With the Chinks* and many good suggestions.

I thank Zhang Yan, of the University of Shandong, and Philip Vanhaelemeersch, visiting scholar of the Hogeschool West-Vlaanderen in Belgium, for their research work.

China Central Television's six-part documentary, broadcast in 2009, aired the official view of the workers.

The Gamble Library of the Union Theological College in Belfast kindly provided access to the reports written by my grandfather, Rev. Frederick O'Neill, who served with the Chinese Labour Corps from 1917 to 1919.

PHOTOGRAPHS

PAGE 34, photograph from Ellen N. LaMotte's *Peking Dust* (New York, 1919); PAGE 46 (bottom) courtesy of The Tank Museum, Bovington, England; PAGES 46 (top), 56 (both images), 69, 83 (both images) all courtesy of In Flanders Fields Museum, Ypres, Belgium.